WORLD RELIGIONS

CHRISTIANITY

John Logan

Wayland

First published in 1995 by
Wayland (Publishers) Ltd,
61 Western Road, Hove,
East Sussex BN3 1JD

This book was prepared for Wayland (Publishers) Ltd
by Ruth Nason

Book design: Alex Latham, Ken Alston

Typeset: A.J. Latham Ltd,
Houghton Regis, Dunstable, Bedfordshire

Printed and bound in Italy by G. Canale & C.S.p.A., Turin

British Library Cataloguing in Publication Data
Logan, John
    Christianity. – (World Religions Series)
    I. Title. II. Series
    200

ISBN 0-7502-1443-0

Acknowledgements

The author thanks the following for their help in preparing the book: Joe Cassidy, Hugh and Marion Crawford, Helen, Clare and Hannah Crawford, Ron Germany, Mary Grey, Andrée Heaton, Margaret, Andrew and Matthew Logan, Andrew and Julie Lunn, Sister Mary John Mananzan, Stephen Need, Sarah Pearce, Danny Sullivan, Stephen Thomas, Angela Wood.

The author and publishers thank the following for their permission to reproduce photographs: The British Library: p. 21; Christian Aid: p. 16 (Jo Jones); Circa Photo Library: cover, pp. 3, 7, 9, 23, 45; EYE UBIQUITOUS: p. 29; Robert Harding Picture Library: pp. 8 (PHOTRI), 13 (bottom) (J.G.Ross); Hutchison Picture Library: pp. 6 (D. Brinicombe), 28 (bottom) (Bernard Régent), 42 (Angela Silvertrop), 44 (bottom); Methodist Church Overseas Division: p. 17 (Rev. M. Austin); Christine Osborne: pp. 14, 27, 34, 39 (bottom), 40; TRIP: pp. 1 (M. Feeney), 4, 5 (top) (O. Semenenko), 5 (bottom) (J. Highet), 10 (R. Cracknell), 13 (top) (D. Macdonald), 15 (top) (M. Lee), 15 (bottom) (N. Price), 24 (I. Burgandinov), 25 (D. Macdonald), 26 (B. Turner), 28 (top) (O. Godow), 30 (A. Tjagny-Rjadno), 31 (J. Filmbase), 32 (top) (P. Ranter), 32 (bottom) (F. Good), 33 (top) (I. Burgandinov), 33 (bottom) (H. Rogers), 36 (top) (O. Godow), 36 (bottom) (R. Musallam), 37 (top) (G. Wittenberg), 37 (bottom) (J. Ringland), 38 (R.Langfield), 39 (top) (J. Wakelin), 41 (Z. Hasasym), 44 (top) (M. Booth).

Cover photo: A baptism in an Anglican church.
Page 1: The figure of Jesus, part of a Holy Week parade in Alicante, Spain.
Page 3: A wall-hanging in a South African church, depicting the resurrection of Jesus.

Contents

INTRODUCTION

AROUND THE WORLD

By the year 2000, it is estimated that the largest numbers of Christians will be in Latin America, followed by Europe, then Africa, North America, Asia and the former USSR.

Christians are people who follow the teachings and example of Jesus Christ, who lived in the land of Israel about two thousand years ago. Most Christians believe that Jesus is the Son of God and, as such, is still alive today.

Jesus came into conflict with the religious authorities of his own time. Eventually he was put to death on a cross. Christians believe that on the third day he rose from the dead. He appeared afterwards to several of his followers and told them to pass on to other people what they had understood from him about God and the Kingdom of God. Later, some of his followers said they saw him ascend into heaven.

Ever since Jesus's first followers began to spread his message, Christianity has been a missionary religion. Today there are Christians world-wide.

The Holy Bible is the main book Christians refer to. It contains stories of the Jewish people, their law and teachings, and then the story of Jesus and the first Christians. The Bible has been translated into almost every language.

Many Christians gather for worship on a Sunday, and to celebrate Christian festivals. At Christmas they give thanks for the birth of Jesus, and at Easter they remember his death on

Jesus: a mosaic in the sixth-century church of St Sophia, Istanbul, Turkey.

A Russian painting of a priest giving holy communion.
The picture conveys the idea of Christians coming together
as a community.

Three main groups
within Christianity are
the Orthodox Church,
the Roman Catholic
Church and the
Protestant Church, and
there are many different
denominations within
each of these.

About 60 per cent of
Christians are Roman
Catholic, 12 per cent are
Orthodox, and 25 per
cent are Protestant.

the cross and rejoice in his resurrection (coming back
to life and living for ever). The ways in which they read
the Bible, worship and celebrate festivals are tremen-
dously varied.

There are over 20,000 different groups or 'denominations' of Christians. These have developed because
Christian communities have disagreed about the cor-
rect way to practise their faith or have claimed that
new experiences have changed their faith in some way.

Christians practise their religion
differently depending on their
denomination and also on where
they live. Some countries claim
to be Christian. In others, being
a Christian is illegal, although

Christians use a variety of ways to
tell people what they believe.
The pictures on the back of this
lorry in Nigeria are one example.

A parade was held to mark the opening of a new Roman Catholic church in Papua New Guinea.

Christians may still be found there. In the past, Christian missionaries went from Europe to countries in Africa, Asia and South America. They introduced not just their religion but also Western styles of worship, church buildings and traditions. Nowadays, the churches in these countries are exploring their Christian faith in the light of their own experience and cultures. They use their own styles of music and worship and some of these have come to influence Christian worship in the West.

When Christians speak of 'church', they may mean the building where they meet for worship, but often they also mean all the people who make up the church community. Members of a church think of themselves as the church 'family'. Christians of all denominations think of themselves as belonging to one main family, the Christian Church. Sometimes they use another image and say that churches around the world, however different they may be, represent 'the body of Christ' in today's world.

1

THE STORY OF CHRISTIANITY

Jesus

Christians trace their roots back to Jesus. He was a Jew who lived in Judea, a province of the Roman Empire, approximately two thousand years ago. Most of the information we have about his life and death comes from accounts thought to have been written by four of his followers, Matthew, Mark, Luke and John. Their accounts, or 'gospels', come at the beginning of the New Testament of the Christian Bible. Each writer tells the story of Jesus in a slightly different way.

Traditional Christian belief is that Mary, the mother of Jesus, was betrothed (engaged) to a carpenter called Joseph. An angel, or messenger from God, spoke to her, telling her that she would 'conceive and give birth to a son'. Matthew and Luke say that Mary became pregnant 'by the Holy Spirit', not by a man. In Luke's account, which is the more detailed, the angel told Mary that the child would be called 'Son of God'.

Little is known of Jesus's childhood. It is assumed that he had a normal Jewish upbringing.

Mary and Jesus, as depicted on a portable Ethiopian icon.

JESUS IN THE TEMPLE

Luke tells a story of how Jesus at the age of twelve went to Jerusalem with his parents for the festival of Passover. On their way home, Joseph and Mary realized that Jesus was not with them. They found him, still in the temple, talking to the Jewish teachers about the Jewish scriptures. The teachers were amazed at his knowledge and understanding. Jesus said 'Did you not know that I was bound to be in my Father's house?'

'Jesus said:

Blessed are the poor in spirit; the kingdom of Heaven is theirs.
Blessed are the sorrowful; they shall find consolation.
Blessed are the gentle; they shall have the earth for their possession.
Blessed are those who hunger and thirst to see right prevail; they shall be satisfied.
Blessed are those who show mercy; mercy shall be shown to them.
Blessed are those whose hearts are pure; they shall see God.
Blessed are the peacemakers; they shall be called God's children.
Blessed are those who are persecuted in the cause of right; the kingdom of Heaven is theirs.'
(Matthew, chapter 5, verses 3–10, *Revised English Bible*)

The teaching of Jesus

Between the ages of thirty and thirty-three, Jesus spent most of his time teaching about the Kingdom of God. One of his most important messages was that poor and oppressed people could enter this Kingdom. In order to convey his ideas, he told stories, called 'parables', about nature and everyday human experience. He gathered a group of twelve people who became known as his 'disciples'. They travelled with him, learned from him, and were his companions in his work.

Before he started teaching, Jesus was baptized in the River Jordan by John the Baptist. Matthew's gospel says that, as Jesus was coming out of the water, a voice from heaven was heard: 'You are my beloved Son; in you I take delight.' This fresco of the baptism of Jesus is from a Greek Orthodox church on Mount Athos, Greece.

The gospels also tell of miracles that Jesus performed. He healed sick people, enabled lame people to walk again, and made blind people able to see. There are even accounts of Jesus bringing people back to life after they had died. Other gospel stories describe how Jesus had power over nature. For example, he calmed a storm, and walked on water.

Jesus's death and resurrection

For most Christians, the greatest miracle happened after the Roman government had put Jesus to death, by crucifixion: two days later he came back to life. This is called the 'resurrection' and, for most Christians, is the centre-point of their faith. Each year, at Easter, they celebrate the resurrection and its importance in their lives.

Some women who went to Jesus's tomb were the first to discover that his body was not there. He had 'risen from the dead'. The gospel writers tell of a number of occasions when Jesus appeared to his followers after his death. He told them to pass on his teaching to others.

The first Christians

Jesus's followers gathered in Jerusalem and prayed together. They believed that Jesus was the Messiah or Christ, whose coming had been foretold by prophets. At the time of the Jewish festival of Pentecost, they were suddenly filled with new hope and had the confidence to start telling others that Jesus was alive.

Christians explain what happened at Pentecost as the coming of the Holy Spirit. The story, which is told in the Acts of the Apostles, includes images of a driving wind filling the house where the followers were, and of tongues of fire resting on each person. People from different nations, who had gathered in Jerusalem for the festival, all heard and understood in their own native language what the disciples said.

The Pentecost experience is often used to mark the birth of Christianity. The first Christians told the good news, or 'gospel', of Jesus Christ, and many more people became his followers. As a sign of their decision to follow Jesus, they were baptized in water.

Greek icon painters are not allowed to show the resurrection of Jesus, but show him raising other people from the dead, to a new life.

'We believe in one
God the Father
All-Sovereign, maker
of heaven and earth,
and of all things visible
and invisible;
And in one Lord
Jesus Christ, the only
begotten Son of God...
And in the Holy Spirit,
the Lord and the
Life-giver, that proceeds
from the Father, who
with the Father and Son
is worshipped together
and glorified together...'

The spread of Christianity

From the time of Pentecost onwards, Christians like
Paul went on missionary journeys to pass on their
beliefs about Jesus. As the religion spread, Christians
began to differ in what they believed, and so a number
of councils met to decide and set down some 'creeds',
or statements of belief, in order to unite Christians
everywhere. A creed accepted at the Council of
Nicaea, in 325 CE, is still used today.

Many churches

Through history there have been many disagreements
between different Christian groups, about beliefs and
practices. Sometimes a disagreement resulted in the
formation of separate churches. Differences between
the Eastern style of Christianity, with its main base in
Constantinople, and the Western style, headed by
Rome, led to the formation of the Orthodox Church
and the Roman Catholic Church.

The Protestant Church came into being after a
German monk, Martin Luther, protested at the way
the Roman Catholic Church had become corrupt.

*The Church of the
Holy Sepulchre in
Jerusalem is built
over the place that is
believed to have
been the site of
Jesus's tomb.*

KEY EVENTS IN THE SPREAD OF THE CHRISTIAN CHURCH

All dates are CE (Common Era). See page 47 for further explanation.
c. = circa (about)

c. 29 - 33   Jesus is crucified.
The beginning of the Christian Church, under the leadership of Peter.
The Roman authorities begin to persecute Christians.

44 - 67   Paul makes four missionary journeys, spreading the gospel in Asia Minor, Cyprus, Greece and Rome, Italy, where he is executed.

330   Emperor Constantine, the first Roman emperor to support Christianity, renames the city of Byzantium 'Constantinople', and makes Christianity the official religion of the Roman empire.

432   Patrick begins missionary work in Ireland.

590 - 604   Pope Gregory organizes missions to France and to England.

800   The Pope crowns Charlemagne 'Holy Roman Emperor' and he promotes Christianity throughout western Europe.

988   Russia, under Vladimir, Prince of Kiev, is converted to Christianity.

1054   The Great Schism between the Eastern and Western parts of the Church, leading to the formation of the Orthodox and the Roman Catholic Churches.

1099- 1244   The Crusades. Christian kings send armies across Europe, towards the land of Israel, to defeat the Muslims and reclaim the Holy Land as Christian territory.

1517   Martin Luther posts his list of complaints about the Church, known as the '95 Theses' on the church door at Wittenberg, Germany. Followers of his ideas become known as Protestants. This is the beginning of what was later called the Reformation.

1620   The Pilgrim Fathers settle in Massachusetts, America.

1646   George Fox organizes the Quaker movement, now known as the Society of Friends.

1682   William Penn, an English Quaker, founds Pennsylvania.

KEY EVENTS IN THE SPREAD OF THE CHRISTIAN CHURCH

1739	Methodism begins, as an independent movement within the Church of England.
1792	The Baptists found the first missionary society in England.
1814	The first Anglican bishop in Asia is consecrated in Calcutta, India.
1817	Robert Moffatt arrives in Africa, to convert people to Christianity, and is followed in 1840 by his son-in-law, David Livingstone.
1865	The first black Anglican bishop is appointed, in Nigeria. The Salvation Army is founded.
1914	Pentecostal churches in North America unite to form the Assemblies of God.
1940	An ecumenical community of monks is founded at Taizé, France.
1948	The World Council of Churches is founded.
1949	US Baptist minister, Billy Graham, begins evangelistic tours.
1961	The Orthodox Churches join the World Council of Churches.
1968	US black minister, Martin Luther King, leader of the civil rights movement, is assassinated.
1969	The first women ministers are ordained in the Methodist Church.
1980	El Salvador's Archbishop Oscar Romero is assassinated for speaking out for social justice.
1986	Desmond Tutu is elected Anglican Archbishop of Capetown, South Africa. In the Philippines, the Roman Catholic Church and other key Christians play a leading role in the 'bloodless revolution' ending the rule of Marcos.
1988	A woman bishop is elected in the Episcopal Church of the USA.
1992	Roman Catholics take part for the first time in an assembly of the Council of Churches for Britain and Ireland.
1994	For the first time, the Church of England ordains women to the priesthood.

The Orthodox Church

Today there are two main branches of the Orthodox Church. The Eastern Orthodox group includes the Russian Orthodox, Romanian Orthodox and Greek Orthodox Churches and the Orthodox Church of America. The smaller, Oriental Orthodox group includes the Ethiopian and Syrian Churches, the Armenian Apostolic Church and the Orthodox Church of India.

Inside a Russian Orthodox church in Arkhangelsk, Russia. Orthodox Christians use icons and candles in their prayer and worship.

The Roman Catholic Church

The Roman Catholic Church sought to convert people to Christianity, and so many countries adopted the Roman Catholic tradition. The leader of the Church is the Pope, or 'Holy Father', who lives in the Vatican City in Rome. He is believed to take the place of Jesus's disciple Peter, who led the first Christians and was the first bishop of Rome.

The Protestant Church

In 1517, Martin Luther pinned a list of his complaints about the Church of his time to the church door at Wittenberg, Germany. People who agreed with his protests became known as Protestants. In Germany they formed the Lutheran Church.

The Protestant Church now includes many different denominations. Some of them are the Anglican, Baptist, United Reformed

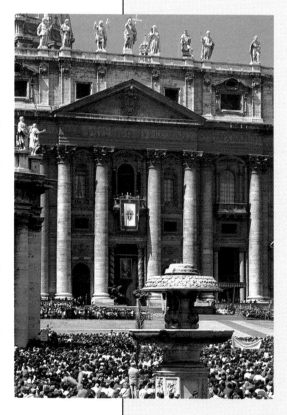

At Easter, crowds gather at the Vatican to hear the Pope speak.

Henry VIII of England wanted a divorce from Queen Catherine, but the Pope would not agree to this. In 1534 Henry therefore left the Roman Catholic Church and declared himself Head of the Church of England. This new denomination developed around the world and is now known as the Anglican Communion.

and Methodist Churches and the Salvation Army. Each has its own way of worshipping, but often the emphasis is on preaching, based on the Bible.

The Pentecostal movement

Many people believe that the experience of 'speaking in tongues' was for the first Christians only, although, throughout history, some people have claimed that they have also had this experience.

At the beginning of the twentieth century, in the USA, small groups of Christians began to pray in different languages and to speak words which they believed were coming directly from God. They called these gifts 'speaking in tongues' and 'prophesying'. From here, the Pentecostal movement grew, particularly in the USA, but also in other countries. Sometimes it is called 'Pentecostal' and sometimes 'Charismatic'.

Some Charismatic Christians stay within their own denomination, such as Roman Catholic or Anglican. Others form their own Community or House Church, often meeting in buildings like school halls for worship. These Christians lay strong emphasis on the Bible as God's Word, and try to live their lives according to what the Bible says.

The Church today

Today the world-wide Christian Church includes many different groups and people, who express their faith in their own ways. Many Christians are encouraging the denominations to communicate with each other and to unite. Different churches hold joint services for worship and contribute together to work in their local community. The movement seeking unity in this way is called the ecumenical movement.

A Church of England priest giving holy communion. The celebration of holy communion should unite Christians everywhere, but often in history it has been the cause of division.

THE WORLD OF CHRISTIANS

2

Christians express their faith in different ways. Many feel it is important to live a Christian lifestyle. This probably means going to church regularly, praying and reading the Bible.

Some Christians choose to use their wealth to help people in need. For other Christians, living a Christian lifestyle means 'evangelizing', or trying to encourage more people to become Christians. Evangelical Christians stress the need to be a 'born-again' Christian and devote their time to gaining new converts and helping them to live in a Christian way.

Some Christians choose a life of struggle. Volunteer workers for organizations such as Christian Aid, CAFOD (Catholic Fund for Overseas Development) and Tear Fund strive to live out their Christian faith by helping where there is great suffering and hardship.

Sometimes, the struggle is for justice. For instance, in the Philippines in 1986, during the Marcos dictatorship, Sister Mary John Mananzan, a Roman Catholic nun, heard that a local shanty town was to be knocked down by bulldozers. This would make many people homeless. She gathered all the sisters together, left a note for their Mother Superior, saying 'Gone to the revolution', and went out to see what she could do. As the bulldozers approached, Sister Mary John laid all the statues of Jesus and Mary that she could find across the road, stood all the pregnant women behind them and then all the nuns behind them. When the drivers of the bulldozers saw this, they turned and went away. It is often in situations similar to this that Christians are trying to make an impact.

St Patrick's Cathedral in Manhattan.

St Jude's Cathedral, Iqualit, Canada.

CHRISTIANITY IN AFRICA

Christianity was present in parts of Africa well before white Westerners arrived to 'convert the pagans'. For example, the Coptic Church of Egypt dates from the sixth century. It now has some 8 million followers.

People in Ethiopia became Christians as early as 300 CE. Today, 60 per cent of Ethiopians belong to the Ethiopian Orthodox Church, which became officially independent in 1959. A distinctive feature of Ethiopian Christian ceremonies is the use of multi-coloured umbrellas, partly to shield people from the sun, but also to symbolize the 'umbrella of peace' (see page 42).

An Ethiopian Orthodox Christian, taking part in a procession at Timket.

In the nineteenth and earlier twentieth centuries Western countries sent missionaries to Africa. They did not understand the different styles of Christianity they found there. For example, African tribal customs had been built in to Christian ceremonies. The missionaries called these customs 'barbaric' and 'primitive'. They tried to preach Western Christianity, and at the same time to impose Western culture.

Many African Christians today are trying to rediscover the original African Christian experience. They are developing their own 'black theology'. Some see a particular link between their own historical experience of slavery and the story in the Bible of Moses helping the people of Israel to escape from slavery in Egypt and leading them to God's 'promised land'. They believe that God wants them to live in the 'promised land of their freedom'. Many black Christians were involved in the struggle to free South Africa from apartheid.

CHRISTIANITY IN SOUTH AMERICA

In South American countries, many people live in extremely poor conditions, in 'favelas' (illegal shanty towns). There is no electricity, and no proper water supply or sanitation. Nonetheless, people feel pride in the homes they build for themselves, out of waste materials.

Christians in such places see the idea that Jesus came to 'bring good news to the poor' and 'set free the oppressed' as particularly relevant. Roman Catholic Christians there have formed into small groups called base communities ('Communidades Eclesiales de Base', or 'CEBs'). As well as meeting for religious services and learning about the Bible, they work to challenge the unjust things that are happening around them. They discuss, for example, how to persuade local leaders to improve the drainage facilities, or whether to farm the land, or how to avoid being beaten by the local police.

Members of the base communities face danger. In El Salvador in March 1980, Archbishop Oscar Romero was assassinated as he was celebrating Mass, along with all the other priests who were present. He was known as a spokesperson for the poor.

Today, increasing numbers of people are joining the evangelical and Pentecostal churches of South America. The Assemblies of God are believed to be the largest Protestant denomination there, with three quarters of a million followers.

These garbage pickers in Brazil stopped for worship with a nun and a minister from their community.

CHRISTIANITY AROUND THE WORLD

The shadings on this map show the main Christian denomination (the one with the largest number of members) in each country.

Countries and, where possible, towns that are mentioned in the book are shown on the map.

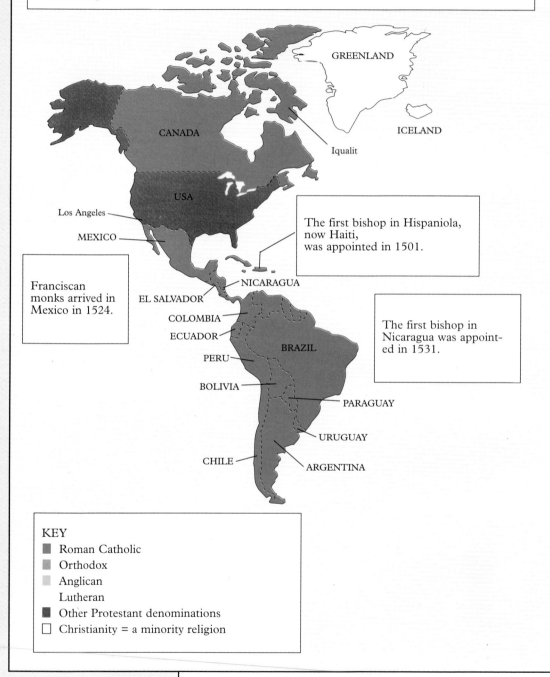

GREENLAND

ICELAND

CANADA

Iqualit

USA

Los Angeles

MEXICO

The first bishop in Hispaniola, now Haiti, was appointed in 1501.

Franciscan monks arrived in Mexico in 1524.

NICARAGUA

EL SALVADOR

COLOMBIA

ECUADOR

BRAZIL

PERU

BOLIVIA

The first bishop in Nicaragua was appointed in 1531.

PARAGUAY

URUGUAY

CHILE

ARGENTINA

KEY
- Roman Catholic
- Orthodox
- Anglican
- Lutheran
- Other Protestant denominations
- ☐ Christianity = a minority religion

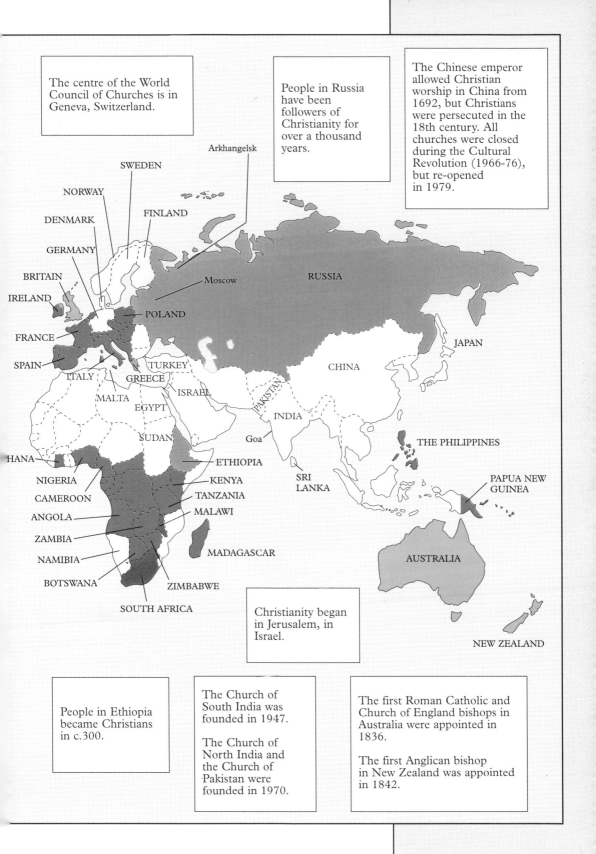

The centre of the World Council of Churches is in Geneva, Switzerland.

People in Russia have been followers of Christianity for over a thousand years.

The Chinese emperor allowed Christian worship in China from 1692, but Christians were persecuted in the 18th century. All churches were closed during the Cultural Revolution (1966-76), but re-opened in 1979.

Arkhangelsk

SWEDEN

NORWAY

FINLAND

DENMARK

GERMANY

BRITAIN

IRELAND

Moscow

RUSSIA

POLAND

FRANCE

JAPAN

SPAIN

TURKEY

CHINA

ITALY

GREECE

MALTA

ISRAEL

EGYPT

PAKISTAN

INDIA

SUDAN

Goa

THE PHILIPPINES

HANA

ETHIOPIA

NIGERIA

KENYA

SRI LANKA

PAPUA NEW GUINEA

CAMEROON

TANZANIA

ANGOLA

MALAWI

ZAMBIA

NAMIBIA

MADAGASCAR

AUSTRALIA

BOTSWANA

ZIMBABWE

SOUTH AFRICA

NEW ZEALAND

Christianity began in Jerusalem, in Israel.

People in Ethiopia became Christians in c.300.

The Church of South India was founded in 1947.

The Church of North India and the Church of Pakistan were founded in 1970.

The first Roman Catholic and Church of England bishops in Australia were appointed in 1836.

The first Anglican bishop in New Zealand was appointed in 1842.

3

60 - 100 Gospels of Matthew, Mark and Luke written.

100 - 200 The Gospel of John probably written.

c.382 Books in Old and New Testaments established.

c.386 Bible translated into Latin.

863 Bible translated into Slavonic.

1388 Latin Bible translated into English by John Wyclif.

1525 New Testament translated into English by William Tyndale.

1611 'Authorized Version' of the Bible published. It was authorized by King James I of England and was the first popular Bible translation.

1804 British and Foreign Bible Society founded, to translate the Bible into as many languages as possible.

THE HOLY BIBLE

The Holy Bible is the main book of the Christian religion. It consists of the Old Testament and the New Testament. The Old Testament is the Bible that Jesus himself would have used. The New Testament tells the story of Jesus and the first Christians.

The Bible Jesus knew

When Jesus talked about the scriptures, he meant the Jewish, Hebrew Bible, which he learned to recite and love. The first part is the 'Torah' (the Jewish teaching), including the story of the creation and of the early ancestors of the Hebrew people, such as Abraham and Sarah, and Moses, who led the people of Israel out of slavery in Egypt. Jesus would have studied the requirements of the Jewish teaching, and in particular he would have learned the words of the 'Shema':

'Hear, Israel: the Lord is our God, the Lord is our one God; and you must love the Lord your God with all your heart and with all your strength.' (Deuteronomy, chapter 6, verses 4 - 6)

As well as the Torah, in the Jewish Bible, there are also the 'Nevi'im' (stories of the prophets, such as Isaiah, Jeremiah, Amos and Hosea) and the 'Ketuvim' (writings, including the Psalms). Christians call all these books of the Bible together the Old Testament.

At first the books of the Old Testament were written on parchments, in the Hebrew language. Copies written in Greek also survived, and these contained some books that were not in the Hebrew version. These extra books are called the 'Apocrypha'. It forms part of the Roman Catholic version of the Bible.

The New Testament

The New Testament is a collection of stories and letters about Jesus and the beginnings of the Christian Church. It was written in the Greek language, by a range of people, some who knew Jesus and some who were converted to Christianity at a later date. It was not until 367 CE that Athanasius, Bishop of Alexandria, put the books and letters in the order that they appear in the New Testament today.

First, there are four accounts of Jesus's life, known as the 'gospels' (the word means 'good news'). The writers are Matthew, Mark, Luke and John, who each tell the story of Jesus, his death and resurrection, in a different way. Luke probably also wrote the book that follows the gospels, called 'The Acts of the Apostles'. It tells the story of the Pentecost experience, and relates how the early Christians went on missionary journeys and how many of them were persecuted.

The letters in the New Testament, sometimes called 'epistles', are believed to have been written by some of the early Christians, such as Paul, to churches in other areas and countries. Sometimes they wrote to encourage Christians who were being persecuted. Sometimes they wrote to reprimand them.

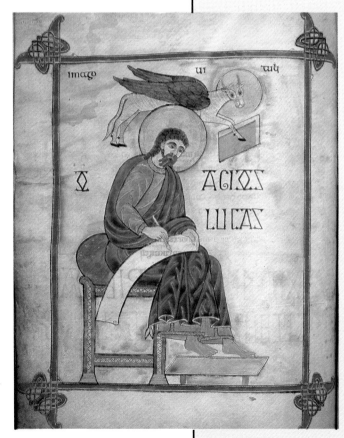

St Luke, as painted in the Lindisfarne Gospels, a copy of the gospels made in the seventh century at the monastery on the island of Lindisfarne. Luke's symbol is the winged calf.

THE PARABLE OF THE SOWER

Jesus told stories, or parables, like the following, to teach people about the Kingdom of God:

'A sower went out to sow. And . . . some of the seed fell along the footpath; and the birds came and ate it up. Some fell on rocky ground, where it had little soil, and it sprouted quickly because it had no depth of earth; but when the sun rose it was scorched, and as it had no root it withered away. Some fell among thistles; and the thistles grew up and choked the corn, and it produced no crop. And some of the seed fell into good soil, where it came up and grew, and produced a crop; and the yield was thirtyfold, sixtyfold, even a hundredfold.'
(Mark, chapter 3, verses 3 - 9)

The people hearing the parable would have grown their own crops, so they would have related easily to the story of the sower. Later, Jesus explained the meaning behind it to the disciples:

'The sower sows the word. With some the seed falls along the foot-path; no sooner have they heard it than Satan comes and carries off the word which has been sown in them. With others the seed falls on rocky ground; as soon as they hear the word, they accept it with joy, but it strikes no root in them; they have no staying-power, and when there is trouble or persecution on account of the word, they quickly lose faith. With others again the seed falls among thistles; they hear the word, but worldly cares and the false glamour of wealth and evil desires of all kinds come in and choke the word, and it proves barren. But there are some with whom the seed is sown on good soil; they accept the word when they hear it, and they bear fruit thirtyfold, sixtyfold, or a hundredfold.'
(Mark, chapter 3, verses 14 - 20, *Revised English Bible*)

Jesus wanted people to understand that, just as the farmer is most pleased when the seed falls on good soil and produces a large crop, so Jesus is most pleased when his teaching about God's Kingdom is heard and remembered by people, for these people then gain a richness and fulness in their lives.

How Christians read the Bible

Many Christians see the Bible as the 'Word of God' and so they try to live their lives entirely by what it says. Some people who see the Bible in this way are known as 'fundamentalists'. They take everything in the Bible as literally true, including the creation of the world in six days. In denominations which hold this view, the main focus of the church service is an address or sermon, where the minister reads some words from the Bible and tries to explain what they say about God and about how people should lead their lives.

Other Christians still claim that the Bible is the 'Word of God', but they also accept it as an ancient document which has remained relevant today. They do not see every story as totally factual, but may interpret it as having a particular message. For example, they see the story of the creation of the world in six days as mythical rather than factual. The truth it conveys is that God is a Creator God.

Some Christians would say that the Bible is only one means of God's Word being heard in the world. They see it as very important, but also think that people need to read the writings of Christian men and women who have lived at different times in history.

For some Christians the Bible needs to be read in the light of their own experiences of poverty and injustice. And there are some who feel that the Bible does not say enough about women and the contributions they have made to the religion. Of course, there are many Christians who would not fit into any of these groups.

In a traditional Anglican church, the 'lectern' or stand from which the Bible is read, is often in the shape of an eagle. The eagle symbolizes the truth of the Bible spreading out like an eagle in flight.

A Russian Orthodox priest holds a prayer rope, called a 'chotki', as he prays.

Other Christian writings

For Christians, the Bible is the most important book, but they also look to a variety of other writings to help them in their faith. Different denominations have their own prayer books. Sometimes these contain set prayers for Christians to recite, such as the Rosary prayer which Roman Catholics recite while holding their rosary beads.

Some Christians read the writings of Christians through the ages, who are sometimes described as 'Saints'. Some examples are St Augustine, St Francis of Assisi, St Thomas Aquinas, Hildegarde of Bingen and Julian of Norwich.

THE LORD'S PRAYER

The disciples asked Jesus to teach them a prayer. Matthew records:

'This is how you should pray:

> Our Father in heaven,
> may your name be hallowed;
> your kingdom come,
> your will be done,
> on earth as in heaven.
> Give us today our daily bread.
> Forgive us the wrong we have done,
> as we have forgiven those who have wronged us.
> And do not put us to the test,
> but save us from the evil one.'

(Matthew, chapter 6, verses 9-13, *Revised English Bible*)

These words, in a slightly different, extended form, are known as the Lord's Prayer. It is recited in church nearly every Sunday. For Christians, God is like a caring parent. They pray to him about their daily needs, represented by 'our daily bread', and they ask him for forgiveness for things they have done wrong. Christians believe that the whole world is 'God's kingdom'. When they pray, 'Your kingdom come', they are expressing their hope that everyone on earth will come to follow God.

4

HOME AND FAMILY LIFE

Christian parents may try to pass on their faith to their children as they go about their daily lives. They may teach them prayers to say at bedtime, and talk to them about the meaning of festivals such as Christmas and Easter. However, there is no specific religious act that needs to be performed at home, and there is no special item that identifies a Christian household. An Orthodox family may have an icon of Jesus or one of the saints, and there may be a small shrine in a Roman Catholic home, but there is no such thing as a typical Christian home or family.

A woman in Arkhangelsk, Russia, reads Bible stories with her granddaughter.

There is a special family custom called 'slava', which is found only in the Serbian Orthodox Church.

SLAVA

In the Serbian Orthodox Church, each family has its own patron saint, who is an intercessor with God for that family: the members of the family believe that the saint talks to God on their behalf.

It is thought that, centuries ago, when people became converted to Christianity, they took the patron saint of the day on which they were baptized as the patron saint for their family. Today, the family saint's day is celebrated at home with feasting and ceremony. This practice is known as 'slava'.

There are five traditional types of prayer:

✝ Praise: telling God how good He is.

✝ Thanksgiving: saying thank you to God for all the good things that have happened.

✝ Penitence: saying sorry to God for the wrongs you have done and asking for His forgiveness.

✝ Supplication: asking God to help you.

✝ Intercession: asking God to help others.

Prayers at mealtimes

Many Christians say a prayer of thanksgiving at mealtimes. This is known as a 'grace'. Two examples are:

'God is Great
God is Good
Let us thank Him for this food.'

'Thank you for the world so sweet,
Thank you for the food we eat,
Thank you God for friends to share,
Thank you God for everything.'

Saying grace.

A prayer which Orthodox Christians may say throughout the day, including before and after meals is:

'Glory be to thee, O Lord, glory to thee. Glory be to thee, O Holy King, that thou hast given us our food to our gladdening; fill us also with thy Holy Spirit, that we may appear before thee well-pleasing and without reproach, for thou hast distributed to each according to his need.'

At mealtimes, Christians may often remember those in the world who do not have enough to eat, or who are suffering in other ways. Some Christian charities encourage people to organize hunger lunches. People come to a meal where very simple food, such as bread, is offered, and they give the money that they might have spent on their normal meal to the charity.

A shrine in a Roman Catholic home in Goa.

Families

Christians celebrate family life, in whatever form that may be. The members of a church are often thought of as one big family, and this can be particularly important for people who have no family, or who are away from home.

Christian charities such as the Children's Society and NCH Action for Children raise money to provide homes and support for children who would otherwise be homeless.

Many Christian families make a special ceremony of lighting the Advent candle on each day of Advent (the period preparing for Christmas).

A church offertory box. Churches use the money people give, to maintain the building and to help carry out their work in the community.

5

CHURCH LIFE

The main day of worship for Christians is Sunday, but the life of a church community goes on throughout the week. People come together for meetings of fellowship or Bible study groups, youth clubs, the Boys' and Girls' Brigades, guides and scouts, choirs, drama societies, sports clubs, and many more. Some meetings may take place in the church buildings and some in people's homes. In some places, churches may run a coffee lounge, a drop-in centre for the unemployed, a parents and toddlers group, and other community services.

At the Crystal Cathedral in Los Angeles, California, the congregation can see the preacher on a video screen.

A church in Sri Lanka. Members of the Early Church, when Christians suffered persecution, used the fish as a secret sign of their faith. Today it is used openly as a Christian symbol.

A CHURCH COMMUNITY IN LEICESTER, ENGLAND

Julie and Andrew Lunn are Methodist ministers in Leicester. They share the job so that they can both look after their two young children. Julie takes responsibility for the largest of their churches, which has about eighty members. About half of them are Afro-Caribbean in origin. 'The church is designed with seating all around, which means that people are able to see each other,' Julie says. 'It is known as a friendly and welcoming church.' They share the church with a local Moravian (another Christian denomination) community and sometimes have joint worship with them.

As part of its service to the community, the church provides free breakfast and supper for the homeless every day. There is also a big Community Project, for which Andrew takes responsibility. He says: 'The project is funded by the local council and employs twenty people who run community activities, including a youth club and a club for children with learning disabilities, called the Wesley Owls. Because Leicester has a large Asian population, the project also tries to meet their needs. There is a Hindu boys' club, and an Asian community worker is employed by the project to develop links with the local community. One day he met a group of Sikh men, who were getting together each day in the park, to play cards. He offered them a place in the church for their meetings instead.'

Andrew is also minister of a small village church with twelve members. He finds there is a real community feeling about the church. Once a month they unite for worship with the local Anglican church.

In any church, the Sunday service usually includes some or all of the following:

☦ The five different kinds of prayer (see page 26).

☦ Readings from the Bible.

☦ Singing of hymns and other songs.

☦ A sermon or homily where the priest, minister or preacher explains more about being a Christian.

☦ An offertory, an opportunity for people to give money to the church.

A Christmas service in Moscow. Orthodox churches are often ornate, full of gold and silver decorations.

Worship

Sunday worship can vary, even within the same church. Services range from solemn to unrestrainedly lively, with every possible variation in between!

Many Christians prefer to worship in a serious, dignified atmosphere. The set words and ceremony and ritual contribute to this. Also, the actual church building has an effect. Worshipping in the majesty of an old cathedral may seem quite different from worshipping in a plain, modern building, even though the form of the service is exactly the same.

For some people, quietness is very important as they pray and listen to God. At a service in a Quaker meeting house, people sit facing each other, thinking and praying in silence, until someone feels that he or she

wants to read from the Bible or another book, or speak about anything he or she wants to.

In churches of some denominations, such as the Methodists and Baptists, the sermon is the main feature of the service. This tradition is reflected in the fact that many old churches have very large pulpits or platforms, from which the minister or leader preaches.

Praying in tongues is an important part of the worship of Charismatic or Pentecostal Christians.

Singers at a Pentecostal church in London.

Nowadays, in some churches of all denominations, other elements are being included in church services, in addition to the traditional prayers, hymns and readings. For example, dance, drama and mime have been introduced, as well as jazz and rock music.

A SOUTHERN BAPTIST CHURCH IN TENNESSEE, USA

'I never really know how long our services are going to last. In my church there are just over 2,000 members and the church is a little like a football stadium. When the worship begins with singing, you can't help but be moved by the sheer noise and excitement of it all. Our worship is often very loud. Sometimes we are very quiet, listening to what God has to say to us. Our pastor takes a Bible passage each week and tries to explain what it has to say to us today. We may be a big church, but we all meet in smaller groups during the week for prayer and more Bible study. I love my church. It helps me to feel God close to me.'
(Suzanne Richards, age 17)

THE CLERGY

The 'clergy' is the general, group name for everyone who is ordained as a minister. In different denominations, ministers are known by different names, such as priests, vicars, pastors, or parsons.

Churches of the same denomination are grouped together in districts, with a senior member of the clergy in charge. In the Roman Catholic, Orthodox and Anglican Churches, this senior clergy person is called a bishop, and the area he is in charge of is a diocese. An archbishop oversees the bishops. The Archbishop of Canterbury is the most senior of all in the Anglican Church.

A Presbyterian minister in Edinburgh, with some of the children from the Sunday School.

Priests and ministers

Some Christians choose to commit their lives to work for the Church. They see their work as a 'vocation', something they are 'called' to do. They may study to become Christian ministers, who will preach the Christian message and care for the community in which they live, thinking especially of people's spiritual well-being. At the end of their training, they are ordained into the ministry.

This minister in Nigeria is called an 'apostle' – a person sent to preach the gospel.

In some sections of Christianity, particularly the Roman Catholic Church, a priest is not allowed to marry, because it is felt that his life should be devoted entirely to serving God. Most denominations allow women to to be ordained into the ministry. The Roman Catholic and Orthodox communities allow only men to be ordained.

Monks and nuns

Some Christians choose to enter a religious order, becoming a monk or a nun. They live in religious communities, governed by particular rules. Some monks and nuns devote themselves to a life of prayer and contemplation, but the majority are involved in pastoral (caring) work in the community, perhaps in schools or hospitals.

Nuns working on a building site in Kazakhstan.

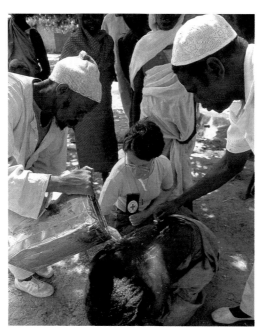

A British nun and two nurses at a leper colony in Sudan.

33

'I believe that the wine I drink actually becomes God within me. Don't ask me how. It's the great mystery of my faith.' (Margarita, a Roman Catholic)

'It helps me to think of Jesus. You see, I believe that Jesus died for me and the bread and wine are symbols which help me think about this.' (David, a Baptist)

'For me the taking of bread and wine is so important. It is then that I meet the living Christ.' (Stefan, a Lutheran)

'In my tradition we don't see the need for outward symbols, such as bread and wine, but through our prayerful silence we find God comes into our lives.' (Olivia, a Quaker)

Holy Communion

Most denominations celebrate Holy Communion, although they do not all call it by the same name. Other names are Eucharist, Mass, the Lord's Supper and the breaking of bread. The Quakers and the Salvation Army are two denominations which do not have a communion service.

A Greek Orthodox priest and congregation in Bethlehem.

At the communion service, Christians remember the story of Jesus sharing bread and wine with his disciples at a Passover meal in the week before he was crucified:

'During supper he took bread, and having said the blessing he broke it and gave it to them, with the words: "Take this; this is my body." Then he took a cup, and having offered thanks to God he gave it to them; and they all drank from it. And he said to them, "This is my blood, the blood of the covenant, shed for many."'
(Mark, chapter 14, verses 22 - 24, *Revised English Bible*)

Christians take Jesus's words to be referring to his suffering on the cross and death, which they believe was necessary to bring 'God's salvation' to the world. Many Christians take communion at important points in their life, such as at their wedding.

6

A CHRISTIAN LIFETIME

Christians see all of life as a gift from God. This idea is present in the ceremonies that mark particular stages in a person's life.

Baptism and initiation

Parents and the Christian community often want to celebrate the birth of a new baby. One of the most usual ways of doing so is through a baptism ceremony. Another name for this is a 'christening'.

The young child is presented in the church, and the parents and congregation make promises to provide a Christian home and lifestyle and to help the child grow up in the Christian faith. The priest or minister either immerses the child in water, or pours water over the child's forehead, sometimes marking the sign of the cross as he speaks the words: 'I baptize you in the name of the Father, and of the Son, and of the Holy Spirit. Amen.' The basin holding the baptismal water is called the font. A lighted candle may be given to the child, as a sign that he or she now 'belongs to Christ' and is part of the Christian community.

The practice of baptism goes back to the time of Jesus, and the first Christians. It is a symbolic washing away of a person's old life without Christ.

A naming angel, from a church in Oldenburg, Germany. The angel's bowl serves as the font, containing the water used at the baptism and naming of a child.

A Palestinian baptism.

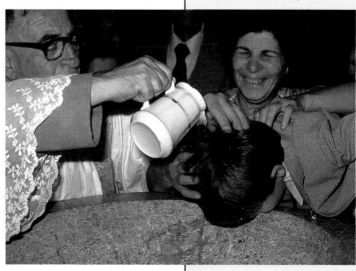

AN ORTHODOX BAPTISM

An ancient ceremony of baptism in the Orthodox Church is full of symbolism. It begins with a prayer. Then the baby's clothes are removed and the baby is submerged in water three times, as a sign of his or her new life as part of the Christian Church. Before the baptism the baby is held facing west, but afterwards east, to show that the child has taken a new direction in life. Three pieces of the baby's hair are cut off, as a sign that he or she belongs to God. Then the baby is anointed or marked with the sign of the cross, with oil (called the 'chrism'), on its forehead, eyes, nostrils, lips, ears, chest, hands, feet. He or she is dressed in new white clothes, as a further mark of his or her 'new life'. A child becomes a member of the Orthodox Church as soon as he or she is baptized, and so the baptism ends with the baby receiving a tiny amount of bread and wine, on a special spoon. A lighted candle is also given to the child.

Some Christian groups, such as Baptist and other evangelical churches, do not baptize babies, but have a service of thanksgiving for the birth. In these churches, people are baptized when they are old enough to make their own decision to commit themselves to following Jesus.

Confirmation

When they feel ready, many Christians, including Anglicans and Roman Catholics, are confirmed. At their confirmation ceremony, they repeat the promises that were made on their behalf when they were baptized as babies. Before people are confirmed, they usually attend a series of confirmation classes.

In the Anglican Church, the ceremony is usually performed by a bishop. He asks:

> 'Do you turn to Christ?
> Do you repent of your sins?
> Do you renounce evil?'

After answering further questions about their beliefs, the confirmands (the people to be confirmed) kneel before the bishop, who lays his hands on each head and says: 'Confirm, O Lord, your servant, with your Holy Spirit.'

Some people take their first Eucharist or Holy Communion at their confirmation ceremony. In the Roman Catholic Church, people usually take their first communion on a separate, earlier occasion.

Believer's Baptism

Denominations which do not baptize babies often have a ceremony called Believer's Baptism. The Baptist Church takes its name from this ceremony, which usually takes place as part of the Sunday service.

In some churches there is a small pool, called a 'baptistry', where the baptism can take place, but it is also quite common for a group from the church to use a local swimming pool, or a river, for the ceremony. The person to be baptized often wears a white robe, as a symbol of purity. When the person is in the water, the minister asks: 'Do you confess Jesus Christ as your Saviour and Lord?' After the response, 'I do,' the minister says: 'I baptize you in the name of the Father and of the Son and of the Holy Spirit.' The person is lowered completely under the water and lifted out again. This is a sign that the 'old life has been washed away' and that the person now 'belongs to Christ'.

Roman Catholic girls in Malta, dressed for their first communion.

Members of the Spiritual Baptist Church conduct a Believer's Baptism.

In the Anglican Church, on the three Sundays before a couple are married, their names and their intention to marry are announced during a church service. This happens at the church where the marriage is to take place, and at the church in the area where each one of the couple lives. It is called 'reading out the banns'.

Marriage

Most Christians choose to marry in a church. In this way, they make their promises 'before God' and ask God to bless their marriage.

At the marriage ceremony, the couple make their vows in front of the congregation. They promise to be faithful to each other all their lives. Then they promise to support each other 'for better, for worse, for richer, for poorer, in sickness and in health, to love and to cherish, till death us do part, according to God's holy law; and this is my solemn vow.'

Many couples choose to take holy communion, as part of their wedding ceremony in church.

In an Orthodox wedding the couple have a silver garland or a garland of flowers placed over their heads, to show the importance of marriage. A prayer is said: 'O Lord God, crown them with glory and honour.' After making their vows, the couple share a cup of wine and walk round the altar three times. In Greek weddings it is traditional for guests to pin money on the bride's dress to wish the couple well.

Death

Christians believe that death is not the end. They believe that when you die, and your body is buried or cremated, your soul lives on with God. The funeral service includes the words: 'I am the resurrection and the life, says the Lord; he who believes in me, though he die, yet shall he live, and whoever lives and believes in me shall not die eternally.'

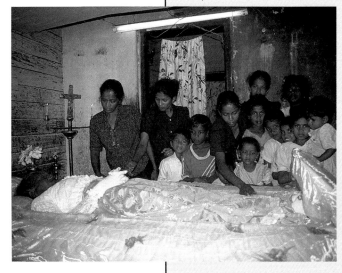

A Roman Catholic funeral in Negombo, Sri Lanka.

For some Christians, especially Roman Catholics, it is important that before a person dies, he or she receives the 'sacrament of the sick'. The priest rubs oil on to the body of the dying person, in the form of a cross. He says a prayer and lays his hands on the person's head. This 'anointing of the sick' is intended to bring comfort to the dying person.

For some Christians, tending the grave of a loved one who has died is an important part of remembering him or her.

A funeral service usually includes prayers, hymns chosen by the dead person's relatives, and a 'eulogy' or speech recalling the good parts of the dead person's life. There are also readings from the Bible, which often include Psalm 23, 'The Lord is my Shepherd'.

At the end of the funeral, the 'committal' takes place. This is when the coffin is lowered into the grave, or put into the furnace for cremation. One example of the words spoken at this part of the ceremony is: 'Forasmuch as our sister/brother has departed out of this life, we therefore commit her/his body to the ground, earth to earth, ashes to ashes, dust to dust, in sure and certain hope of the resurrection to eternal life through our Lord Jesus Christ, to whom be glory for ever and ever. Amen.'

7

SOME SAINT'S DAYS

17 March
St Patrick – took Christianity to Ireland in the fifth century.

16 April (18 February in France)
St Bernadette of Lourdes – had visions of the 'Blessed Virgin Mary' in 1858 CE.

11 August
St Clare of Assisi – founded the 'Poor Clares'.

4 October
St Francis of Assisi – founded the monastic order of Franciscans. He regarded the whole of God's creation as his family. He died in 1126 CE.

6 December
St Nicholas – fourth-century bishop of Myra (in south-western Turkey). In Germany, Holland and Austria, he is said to leave presents of fruit, nuts and sweets in people's shoes.

FESTIVALS

Only some of the main Christian festivals are described here. In fact, hundreds of Christian festivals are celebrated through the year. Every day is a saint's day. Many festivals are celebrated only by particular groups of Christians. There are 'Days of Obligation' which Roman Catholics and Orthodox Christians are expected to observe, for example.

Christmas is the festival that many people associate with Christianity. For many Christians, however, Holy Week and Easter have a deeper significance.

Midnight mass on Christmas Eve at the Lutheran Church of the Redeemer in Jerusalem.

Some Christian festivals fall on the same date every year. Others are movable. Easter Day, for example, can be as early as 22 March or as late as 25 April. Orthodox Christians in Eastern countries use a different calendar from the one used in the West. For Orthodox Christians, the dates of fixed festivals are thirteen days after the dates given here.

September or October HARVEST

Traditionally, this was a time of thanksgiving for a good crop. It is not necessarily a Christian festival, but many Christian churches hold a harvest celebration.

1 November ALL SAINTS' DAY

This festival celebrates all those who provide saintly examples of the Christian faith. It is sometimes known as 'All Hallows'. The day before is 'All Hallows Eve' or 'Hallowe'en'.

November–December ADVENT

The period of Advent, preparing for Christmas, begins four Sundays before Christmas Day. The beginning of Advent marks the beginning of the Christian year.

8 December THE FEAST OF THE IMMACULATE CONCEPTION

This festival is devoted to Mary, the mother of Jesus. It is celebrated mainly by Roman Catholics.

25 December CHRISTMAS DAY

The day on which most Christians celebrate the birth of Jesus.

A harvest celebration in Wroclaw, Poland. The priest is sprinkling holy water.

41

A procession in Ethiopia, to celebrate Epiphany.

6 January EPIPHANY
This festival commemorates the visit of the three wise men from the East to see Jesus.

2 February CANDLEMAS
This festival celebrates the presentation of the baby Jesus in the temple, and the purification of the Blessed Virgin Mary.

February or March SHROVE TUESDAY
Traditionally Shrove Tuesday is the day to be 'shriven' – which means to have all the fats in the house eaten up before the Lenten fast begins. In Britain this is Pancake Day. In some countries this is the time for the Mardi Gras celebration.

February or March ASH WEDNESDAY
The first day of Lent, a time of fasting which traditionally lasts until Holy Week. On this day many Christians go to church to be 'ashed'. A cross is marked on their foreheads with a paste made from the ashes of palm crosses. During the service, the palm crosses from the previous year are burned, ready to make more paste.

February or March to April LENT

A period of forty days during which Christians prepare to hear the Easter story again. The forty-day period also recalls the time when Jesus went into the desert wilderness to think, and was tempted.

March MOTHERING SUNDAY

This festival has its roots in the Roman feast of Matronalia. In the eighteenth and nineteenth centuries, domestic servants in Britain were given a day off to visit their mothers, and would often take a simnel cake (a fruit cake covered with marzipan) as a present. Another custom was for people to visit their 'mother church'. The day was also known as 'Refreshment Sunday' – a day off from the Lenten fast.

March or April PALM SUNDAY

Palm Sunday is the first day of 'Holy Week', which leads up to Easter Day. Christians remember the story of Jesus riding into Jerusalem on a donkey. People waved palm branches to welcome him.

Many churches today hold Palm Sunday processions and re-enact the story with the waving of branches. Small palm crosses may be given out to the congregation.

March or April MAUNDY THURSDAY

On the Thursday of Holy Week Christians remember the last meal Jesus had with his disciples. He shared bread and wine with them, saying 'This is my body' and 'This is my blood'. This story has lived on in the custom of celebrating Holy Communion (page 34). Also at this last supper, Jesus is said to have washed his disciples' feet. He did this as a sign of humility. Roman Catholic popes have always washed the feet of twelve people on Maundy Thursday, in remembrance of this.

The supper was also the occasion when Jesus told the disciples that one of them was going to betray him.

JESUS IN THE WILDERNESS

After Jesus had been baptized by John the Baptist and before he began to teach, he went into the wilderness to think.

'For forty days and nights he fasted, and at the end of them he was famished. The tempter approached him and said, "If you are the Son of God, tell these stones to become bread." Jesus answered, "Scripture says, 'Man is not to live on bread alone, but on every word that comes from the mouth of God.' (Matthew, chapter 4, verses 2-4, *Revised English Bible*)

Processing with the cross in Jerusalem on Good Friday.

March or April
GOOD FRIDAY

Good Friday is the most solemn day of the Christian year, when Christians remember the death of Jesus on the cross. Jesus was made to carry his cross to Calvary Hill, where he would be crucified. On Good Friday mornings, some Christians march together, in the place where they live, as witness to that event. They may carry wooden crosses themselves. Some Christians fast during this day. In the Roman Catholic Church people say prayers in front of each of the 'Stations of the Cross'. These are pictures or sculptures of Jesus carrying his cross to Calvary Hill.

In some parts of the Orthodox Church, the priest brings in an icon of Jesus's body and people stand around it, as though they are at a funeral.

March or April HOLY SATURDAY

Easter Saturday marks the end of Lent. Many Christians prepare to celebrate the resurrection of Jesus on the following day.

In the Philippines people re-enact the story of the crucifixion, and actually tie a person representing Jesus to a cross.

CHRIST IS RISEN!

In the Russian Orthodox and other Orthodox Churches, a vigil begins at midnight on Easter Saturday. The story of the resurrection is re-enacted. A big procession of people move round the outside of the church, as if they are looking for the body of Jesus. As they look, they chant quietly and thoughtfully. When they approach the doors of the church, the priests and deacons say the words that the first women to visit Jesus's tomb are thought to have said: 'They have taken the Lord out of the tomb and we do not know where they have laid him.'

The doors of the church open, symbolizing the rolling away of the stone, and someone asks the question: 'Whom do you seek?' The people reply, 'The body of Jesus.' The answer comes: 'Then why do you search among the dead for one who is alive? He is not here. He is risen.'

The cry of 'Khristos voskrese!' ('Christ is risen!') breaks out and the people respond, 'Voistinu voskrese!' ('is risen indeed'). One by one the people all light a candle called a Paschal candle, until the whole church is full of light.

March or April EASTER SUNDAY

In churches on Easter Sunday, joyful Easter hymns and songs are sung, and in some places a Paschal candle is lit. This burns for forty days after Easter, until the Feast of the Ascension. Some Christians choose to celebrate Easter Sunday by climbing a mountain and holding a dawn service on the summit.

May or June ASCENSION DAY

This occurs forty days after Easter Sunday. Christians remember the time when Jesus, who had risen from the dead and appeared again among some of his followers, finally 'ascended' into heaven to be with God.

May or June PENTECOST

Christians remember the coming of the Holy Spirit, and the beginning of the Church.

For many, Easter is a time for giving eggs, a symbol of the resurrection of Jesus and of new life. These beautiful hand-painted eggs are from Russia.

Glossary

Anglican Church
a Protestant denomination, with its origins in the Church of England. The religious leader of the Anglican Church is the Archbishop of Canterbury.

apostle
a person who was sent out to preach the Christian message.

cathedral
the main church in a diocese, containing the bishop's throne ('cathedra').

Celtic
of the Celts, people inhabiting Wales, Scotland and other parts of Britain and north-west France.

Christ
a title given to Jesus. It means 'the anointed one', meaning the special leader sent by God, as had been promised. 'Christ' is the Greek form of the Hebrew 'Messiah'.

consecrate
to make holy.

contemplation
quiet thought, prayer and meditation. Some Christians live a completely contemplative life.

creed
a statement summing up beliefs.

crucifixion
the most common method of execution used by the ancient Romans. The person was nailed to a cross until he died of suffocation.

diocese
the area under the care and authority of a bishop.

Episcopal Church
the Anglican Church in the USA, governed by its own bishops.

evangelize
to tell people the 'good news' of Christianity.

gospel
the 'good news' of Christianity. The belief that Jesus came to bring new life. There were traditionally four gospel writers, Matthew, Mark, Luke and John.

Holy Spirit
the power of God in the world today. Christians believe that the Holy Spirit is the third part of God in the Trinity. They believe that it lives in them, giving them strength to practise their faith.

hymn
a song used in worship.

icon
a painting or, sometimes, a mosaic of Jesus, Mary or one of the saints. Icons are used to aid worship, especially in the Orthodox Church.

liturgy
an order of service for worship. In the Orthodox Church, it means Holy Communion.

mass
Roman Catholic term for Holy Communion.

Messiah
See 'Christ'.

missionary
traditionally, a person who took the Christian message to another country. Nowadays, missionaries work in all sorts of situations, such as hospitals, schools, and engineering projects.

Nonconformist
a name for several Protestant denominations, such as the Baptists and Methodists, who separated from the Church of England.

ordination	a ceremony at which someone is ordained, that is, made a minister or priest.
parable	a story in which something difficult to understand is compared with something in people's everyday lives. Jesus used parables to talk about the Kingdom of God.
Pentecost	the Jewish festival of Weeks. Christians believe that it was on this day, a few weeks after Jesus's death, that his followers first received the Holy Spirit.
Reformation	the movement of religious change that led to the beginning of the Protestant Church.
resurrection	the rising from the dead and living for ever of Jesus. Also, the new life that Christians believe Jesus brings for them.
saint	a person who has lived an exceptionally holy life and whom the Church has officially declared to be a figure for Christians to revere.
theology	the study of God's ('Theos') Word ('Logos'). The study of religion and belief in God.
Trinity	the threefold nature of God – Father, Son and Holy Spirit.
Vatican	the home of the Pope and centre of the Roman Catholic Church. It is a small country within the city of Rome, Italy.

Book List

Bibles and Bible stories
The Good News Bible (Bible Society/HarperCollins) is probably the easiest translation to read.
The Revised English Bible (Oxford University Press/ Cambridge University Press) has been used for some of the Bible pieces quoted in this book.
Pat Alexander, *The Young Puffin Book of Bible Stories* (Puffin, 1988) is an inexpensive and readable collection.
Selina Hastings, *The Children's Illustrated Bible* (Dorling Kindersley, 1993) is a readable and highly illustrated collection of Bible stories.
Meryl Doney, *How The Bible Came To Us* (Lion, 1985) describes how the Bible developed into its present form.
P. Wilkinson, *Eyewitness Guides: Bible Lands* (Dorling Kindersley, 1991) gives a colourful description of what life might have been like in Bible times.

The history of Christianity
T. Dawley, *The History of Christianity* (Lion, 1990).

People
Halcyan Blackhouse, *Corrie Ten Boom* (Hunt and Thorpe, 1992) tells the dramatic story of a Christian woman who hid Jews during the Second World War.
Cyril Davey, *Mother Teresa* (Hunt and Thorpe, 1992) tells the life story of Mother Teresa and her work among the poor in India.
Oliver Hunkin (arranged), *Dangerous Journey: The Story of Pilgrim's Progress* (Candle Books/Eerdman, 1994) is a lovely retelling of John Bunyan's *Pilgrim's Progress*.
The John Wesley Story (Methodist Publishing House, 1987) is a vivid cartoon story of the founder of the Methodist Church.

Fiction
A wide range of stories and novels about Christians and Christianity can be found in specialist Christian book-shops. One classic of Christian fiction is C.S. Lewis, *The Lion, the Witch and the Wardrobe*. It is an allegorical tale of the Easter story.

Note on Dates

Each religion has its own system for counting the years of its history. The starting point may be related to the birth or death of a special person or an important event. In everyday life, today, when different communities have dealings with each other, they need to use the same counting system for setting dates in the future and writing accounts of the past. The Western system is now used throughout the world. It is based on Christian beliefs about Jesus: AD (Anno Domini = in the year of our Lord) and BC (Before Christ). Members of the various world faiths use the common Western system, but, instead of AD and BC, they say and write CE (in the Common Era) and BCE (before the Common Era).

Index